Reduce Anxiety,
Increase Focus, and
Spark Creativity

mindfulness
Coloring Book
for Teens

callisto
publishing
an imprint of Sourcebooks

Copyright © 2022 by Callisto Publishing LLC
Cover and internal design © 2022 by Callisto Publishing LLC
Illustrations © 2021 Collaborate Agency

Art Director: Diana Haas
Art Producer: Hannah Dickerson
Editor: Laura Apperson
Production Editor: Caroline Flanagan
Production Manager: Holly Haydash

Callisto Teens and the colophon are registered trademarks of Callisto Publishing LLC.

Published by Callisto Publishing LLC C/O Sourcebooks LLC
P.O. Box 4410, Naperville, Illinois 60567-4410
(630) 961-3900
callistopublishing.com

Printed and bound in the United States of America.

PAH 10 9 8 7 6 5 4 3

This coloring book
belongs to

_____

Introduction

Welcome to your mindfulness coloring book! Practicing mindfulness means focusing your awareness on what you're feeling and experiencing, without judging that experience. Studies have shown that coloring is a great mindfulness practice, as it reduces stress and focuses your mind on the present moment. It promotes patience and creativity, allows you to make art without judgment, helps you embrace imperfection, and soothes anxious thoughts.

The goal of this book is to help you find your flow and relax as you celebrate your own unique style of creative expression. The illustrations promote a sense of positivity, balance, and serenity—so clear your mind, focus on your colors of choice, and let your individual personality shine. Whether you've colored in the lines or gone wild, what's important is that you've taken the time to invest in your well-being and peace of mind.

There's no wrong way to use this book. With 35 calming illustrations ranging from simple to complex, there's a page for all occasions. Flip to a page that looks fun to you, and use your colored pencils, fine-tip markers, gel pens, or other chosen art supplies. Keep the pages for yourself or share them with friends—it's up to you. Happy coloring!